AF321716

In Loving Memory

In Loving Memory

In Loving Memory

In Loving Memory

In Loving Memory

In Loving Memory

In Loving Memory

In Loving Memory

In Loving Memory

In Loving Memory

In Loving Memory

In Loving Memory

In Loving Memory

In Loving Memory

In Loving Memory

In Loving Memory

In Loving Memory

In Loving Memory

In Loving Memory

In Loving Memory

In Loving Memory

In Loving Memory

In Loving Memory

In Loving Memory

In Loving Memory

In Loving Memory

In Loving Memory

In Loving Memory

In Loving Memory

In Loving Memory

In Loving Memory

In Loving Memory

In Loving Memory

In Loving Memory

In Loving Memory

In Loving Memory

In Loving Memory

In Loving Memory

In Loving Memory

In Loving Memory

In Loving Memory

In Loving Memory

In Loving Memory

In Loving Memory

In Loving Memory

In Loving Memory

In Loving Memory

In Loving Memory

In Loving Memory

In Loving Memory

9 781912 817108